MW00588043

AN OUTLINE OF CINYANJA GRAMMAR

DOROTHEA A. LEHMANN

Series Editor: MUBANGA E. KASHOKI

Bookworld Publishers

Published by Bookworld Publishers
PO Box 32581, Lusaka, Zambia.
2002

Reprinted in 2013

Copyright Institute of Economic and Social Research 2002

All rights reserved. No part of this publication may be reproduced, stored in a retrieval system, or transmitted, in any form or by any means electronic, mechanical, photocopying, recording or otherwise, without the prior permission of the publisher.

ISBN 9982 24 0153

Typesetting by Fergan Limited, Lusaka, Zambia.
Printed by Printech Limited, Lusaka, Zambia.

FOREWORD

There has been a lack of up to date descriptive grammars of Zambian languages suitable for use, either as teaching or as learning aids, at all levels of the Zambian education system. This lack has been keenly felt by teachers and learners alike. Many of the grammars that are available could be said to be inadequate or inappropriate in several respects. The oldest ones were written at a time when Latin or European languages generally were considered to be the prototype of all grammars, and thus they tended to be patterned in their arrangement, description and the terminology employed on Latin-based grammatical rules. Others were written in a style and language which presented serious problems of comprehension even to teachers. In a good many cases, the actual examples cited were unnatural, forced or not in accord with accepted usage. At the present moment many of these works have long been out of print.

In order to put in the hands of the teachers and learners grammatical descriptions which reflected more nearly the structural facts of their language, during 1970-71, the Survey of Language Use and Language Teaching in Zambia attempted to provide comprehensible grammatical descriptions of the seven Zambia languages officially prescribed for use in education, broadcasting and literacy programmes. The authors who volunteered or were approached to write them were specifically instructed to employ a comprehensible style and to keep technical terminology to the absolute minimum. The general reader was clearly in mind. It is hoped that with the publishing now of the grammatical outlines of iciBemba, siLozi, ciNyanja and iciTonga the original intention of providing grammatical descriptions of appeal to a wide audience, both lay and professional, will have been achieved.

As originally conceived, seven grammatical sketches representing all the seven officially approved Zambian languages, plus sketches of Town Bemba and Town Tonga, were to have been published as Part One in a projected three-part volume of **Language in Zambia,** incorporating the findings of the Zambia Language Survey. In the event, it was found necessary in the interest of reducing bulk and cost to abandon the original plan and to arrange to publish the sketches separately. Indeed, publishing them separately has the advantage of making them available in a convenient, less bulky size suitable for both teacher and student handling.

The Institute for African Studies (now the Institute of Economic and Social Research), University of Zambia, published in 1977 **Language in Zambia: Grammatical Sketches,** Volume 1, containing grammatical sketches or outlines of iciBemba and kiKaonde by Michael Mann and JL Wright respectively, plus a sketch of the main characteristics of Town Bemba by Mubanga E Kashoki. The plan at the time was to publish subsequently two follow-up volumes: first, Volume 2, to contain sketches of siLozi and Lunda and Luvale and second, Volume 3, to contain sketches of ciNyanja and iciTonga. In the event this plan was not adhered to. Only one volume was published in accordance with the original plan and this has been out of print for some time now.

It is in part for these reasons that it has been considered necessary to attend to the unfinished business initiated some two decades ago. Also, and more pertinently, the need for pedagogical and reference grammars of Zambian languages continues to be keenly felt. The matter has now been made more urgent following the recent (1996) decision of the Zambian Government to revert to the earlier policy of using local (i.e. Zambian) languages plus English as a media of instruction. As now re-arranged, in order to achieve what is felt to be a more logical arrangement, four grammatical sketches of iciBemba, siLozi, ciNyanja and iciTonga have been published.

Co-sponsored by the Institute for African Studies, (the present Institute of Economic and Social Research, University of Zambia), the main volume, **Language in Zambia,** was published in 1978 by the International African Institute (IAI) partly subsidised by funds from the Ford Foundation. The Institute gratefully acknowledges the permission granted by the Foundation, the sponsors of the language survey of which the material published herein is a partial outcome, to have the sketches published separately. Gratitude is also due to the authors of the sketches for their contribution in a field in which much remains to be done.

Other acknowledgements are due to Bookworld Publishers for publishing the sketches in collaboration with the Institute; to the editors of **Language in Zambia,** Sirarpi Ohannessian and Mubanga E Kashoki, for carrying out the bulk of the necesssary initial editorial work; to Dr. Tom Gorman who was detailed to bring a general stylistic consistency to the sketches; and to the secretarial Institute staff for preparing the typesrcipt. Above all, the eventual publication of the sketches owes much to the Zambian Government, in particular the Ministry of Education, and to the University of Zambia for their interest and support and for providing a conducive environment in which fruitful research work could take place during the life of the Survey of Language Use and Language Teaching in Zambia.

Mubanga E Kashoki
Professor of African Languages
INSTITUTE OF ECONOMIC AND SOCIAL RESEARCH
UNIVERSITY OF ZAMBIA
EDITOR

INTRODUCTION

In the population census of 1969 nearly 700,000 residents of Zambia registered ciNyanja or languages and / or dialects related to it as their mother tongue[1]. They form after the Bemba-speaking population the second largest language group in the country. It is estimated that a quite sizeable number of people use ciNyanja as their second language since, besides other factors, the language has been taught for a long time in primary and secondary schools in Lusaka and the Eastern Province[2]. It still is to a certain extent the lingua franca of the armed forces and the police and is used is used by the Zambia Government in official publications and radio broadcasts. Nyanja (ciNyanja) is the name used for a group of dialects spoken in Zambia, Malawi and Mozambique. The name originated from the 'Lake Nyanja', the language being spoken by peoples of Likoma island and the eastern shore of Lake Malawi. The Manjanja of southern Malawi and the Cewa of the west and southwest of the lake and the Eastern Province of Zambia have much greater numbers of speakers. The then President of Malawi therefore decided in 1969 that the official language of Malawi should be ci-Chewa (spelt Chichewa by Presidential decree). This name is also the most appropriate for the language spoken by the Zambians of the Eastern Province. They call themselves a-Cewa, 'the Cewa people'. Recordings made in the Katete District of Zambia and in Lusaka show great similarities in phonology, grammar and vocabulary to the Cewa studies (See bibliography).

Overall, school text-books in Zambia are mainly based on Manjanja, a language which gained prestige through several early publications, such as the *Dictionary of the Nyanja Language* by Scot and Hetherwick based on an earlier

---

[1.] The 1980 Census of population and Housing estimated the Cinyanja-speaking population to be 17.6% of the total population.
[2.] Ohannessian, Sirarpi and Mubanga E. Kashoki, *Language in Zambia*.

Cyclopaedic Dictionary of the Manjanja Language by DC Scott (1892), and the *Practical Manual of the Nyanja Language* by A Hetherwick (1904). Accepting these books as authorities, teachers are apt to fall into self-concious spelling pronunciations and unidiomatic school phraseology when questioned about the language. Standardisation has not yet been achieved with the various dialect groups struggling against the strait jacket of the official *Chinyanja Orthography Rules* of 1931[1] and the later amendment efforts of these. A union Nyanja version was used in the translation of the Bible published by the Bible Societies of Central Africa. It is aimed at using a language and an orthography which can be understood by all who speak a local dialect or a town version of Nyanja. The present short outline is mainly based on the ciNyanja used in formal teaching in Zambian schools and in publications as well as that to be found in recordings made in the Katete District and in Lusaka.

ACKNOWLEDGEMENTS*

My sincere thanks are due to Mr. S.E. Kawinga of Chassa Secondary School, Rev. Sakala of Katete Secondary School and Father N. Salaun of Likuni Language Centre for their generous help with this study, and to Professor G. Fortune for his careful revision of the first draft. Since I have not always followed their suggestions all remaining mistakes are my own fault.

---

[1] Standardisation was attempted in 1977 with the publication of Zambian Languages: *Orthography Approved by the Ministry of Education.* (Neczam. 1977).

* This work is being published posthumously, several years after the authors death in her native Germany. It was written while she was still a Senior Research Fellow of the University of Zambia at the then Institute for African Studies, now the Institute of Economic and Social Research (Editor).

Chapter 1

THE SOUND SYSTEM OF CINYANJA

THE VOWELS

Table 1

	Front	Central	Back
High	i		u
Mid	e		o
Low		a	

Cinyanja has five contrastive or distinctive vowels which occur in short or long duration. The following verb stems, when contrasted one with another, form pairs which differ only in the quality of the vowels.

e.g. *-pinda*   'fold'   *-penda*   'count'

-panda   'beat'   *-ponda*   'tend'

-punda   'name'

Words of identical shape with different meanings may have a contrast in vowel length. Double letters (i.e. the writing of the same vowel letter twice) are used in this outline to indicate length. [This device is now used following the 1977 officially approved orthography of Cinyanja].

e.g. *mbale*   'plate'   *mbaale*   'brother'

-bvika   'thatch'   *-bviika*   'dip in water'

-fula   'dig out'   *-fuula*   'shout'

1

Extra long vowels are characteristic of ideophones and interjections

e.g.   *eee*   'yes'

        piii   'very hard'

        phaa phaa phaa   'rising like dust'

        thoo   'very full'

        puu   'sound of pouring water'

Fusion and Elision of Vowels

The juxtaposition of two vowels in Cinyanja is common. When two vowels of the same quality come together they are fused into one long vowel,

e.g.   *kumbukani ici* 'remember this' is pronounced *kumbukaniici:* the first syllable of the second word is used with the last syllable of the first word.

This also occurs with infixes,

e.g.   *mtengo a-u-umira* (gloss, the price he-it-raises), meaning 'he increased the price' is pronounced *mtengo auumira*.

An elision of the vowel *i* before a vowel of a different quality is seen in the following two examples where **ndi-** 'I' and **ti** 'we' have no *i* before the tense marker **-a-**,

e.g.   *ndadya* 'I have eaten'   *taona* 'we have seen'.

Noun prefixes and concords (see Table III) show similar elisions:

e.g.   **zi**-*nthu* **z**-*ace* (from **zi**-*ace*) 'his things',

        ci-*manga* **c**-*onse* (from **ci** *onse*) 'all the maize'.

A few cases show a fusion of two vowels of different quality,

e.g.   *a+i* becomes *ee*,

         u+o becomes *oo*,

         a+o becomes *oo*.

The examples below seem to indicate that these are dialectical versions or even borrowed structural patterns from other Bantu languages,

e.g.   *midzi ya-i-kulu* or *yee-kulu* 'big villages'

         mw-ini wamunda 'the owner of the garden' which in the plural becomes

         eeni (a-ini) aminda 'owners of the gardens'

         mu-nthu oonse 'everybody'.

The Final Vowels of a Syllable Ending in -*i* and -*u*

These in many cases occur as *y* and *w* before next vowel, e.g. in noun prefixes and concords:

e.g.   *mw-ana (mu-ana)*   'child'

         mw-ezi (mu-ezi)   'moon'

         my-ulu (plural of *mu-ulu*)   'heaps'[1]

THE CONSONANTS

Table II

	Labial	Alveolar	Palatal	Velar
Voiceless stops	*P*	*t*	*ty*	*k*
Aspirated	*ph*	*th*		*kh*
Affricates	*pf*	*ts*	*tsh=c*	

---

[1] Hetherwick's dictionary notes, for example, that "extra nouns in *mu-* not found here, see under *mw-*; that *mua-, mui-, muo-* will be found *mwa-, mwe-, mwi-, mwo-*," and that "in words beginning with a vowel following the sound *mi-*, one may spell it either with or without *y*: e.g. *myendo*, 'legs', or *miendo*, or *miyendo*, are all heard just as *mu-* has *mwi-, mui-, muwi-*".

	Labial	Alveolar	Palatal	Velar
Aspirated			*thsh=ch*	
Fricatives	*f*	*s*		
Voiced Stops	*b*	*d*	*dy*	*g*
Affricates	*bv*	*dz*	*dzh=j*	
Fricatives	*v*	*z*		
Laterals		*l(r)*		
Nasals	*m*	*n*	*ny*	*n=ng'*
Approximants	*w*		*y*	

Cinyanja orthography uses the letter *-h-* after the voiceless stops to indicate aspiration. Note however that the letters *sh* and *zh* represent sounds similar to the sounds in the English words **shame** and **version**. The official orthography now makes a distinction between the aspirated and the unaspirated palatal affricate. However, in practice both are still spelt *ch* though they are two different phonemes, i.e. they can make the only difference in two otherwise identical words of different meanings (See below).

In writing, *y* after *t*, *d* and *n* is used to differentiate the palatal from the alveolar sounds. while *ŋ* or *ng'* is the alternate spelling for the sound corresponding in English pronunciation with si**ng**ing.

The following examples show groups of words which differ only in the first consonants in shape but are of completely different meanings:

Labials   **Alveolars**

-pa   'on, at'   *-tenga*   'bring, take'

-pha	'kill'	-thenga	'come to stay'
-pfa	'spurting out'	...ga	'trick'
-fa	'die'		'inform'
ba	'steal'		'roof'
va	'wide open (as door)'		'fill'
bala	'bear'	-zaza	'be wild'
-bvala	'clothe; wear; put on'		
mala	'nest of a rat'	dzimba	'smell'
-wala	'shine (sun, moon)'	-zimba	'fade'
		-limba	'be firm, hard'
		linga	'stockade'
		ninga	'as if'

Sell your sellbacky Go to sellb and get an quote. We ipping -

Palatals

-tyoka	'break'
-coka	'go away'
-ca	'ripen'
-cha	'make a noose'
-dyera	'excel'
-chera	'set a trap'
-jenya	'make notches in wood'
-nyenya	'crumble'

Velars

-koma	'be good'
-khoma	'wall'
-goma	'hit'
ŋoma	'drum'

5

-nyira	'make honey'
-nra	'be light, white'

The Nyanja varieties of the different regions vary in the kind and number of contrasting consonants they use. The ciChewa of the Kasungu district in Malawi, which Watkins described (see Bibliography), has fricatives *f* and *v* in words which have the affricates *pf* and *bv* in other regional varieties,

e.g. **Elsewhere**   **Kasungu**

pfinya	'press'	*finya*
pfuula	'shout'	*fuula*
bvina	'dance'	*vina*
bvunda	'rot'	*vunda*
pfupa	'a bone'	*fupa*

Similar dialect variations of *ts* and *s*, *dz* and *z* are heard as well, as noted in Hetherwick's Dictionary:

e.g.
tsegula	'open'	*segula*
dziwa	'know'	*ziwa*

TONES AND INTONATION

Cinyanja uses differences in the pitch levels in which the vowel of a syllable or a syllable nasal is pronounced to indicate differences in the meaning of a word or grammatical item like a tense/aspect marker. In the lexical form a word can be marked carrying a high (´) or low (`) tone on each syllable,

e.g.   *mphùnzìtsì* (all low) 'a teacher'   *nyùmbá* (low/high) 'a house'

   máwà (high/low) 'tomorrow'   *nkúkù* (high/low) 'chicken'

   kùyámkùlà (low/high/low/low) 'to speak'

6

Some words have the same phonetic shape but different tone patterns:

e.g.   *mtèngò* 'price'   *mténgò* 'tree'

          kútì 'where'   *kùtì* 'to say'

          ndì 'is, are'   *ndí* 'with'

Not all the tone patterns of particles and words are stable: some may change with emphasis or according to the pattern of intonation of the whole sentence. The final syllable of a statement is usually low, and the syllable before the final one, the last but one, whether high or low, gets a falling, downgliding tone (ˆ),

e.g.   *tìlì bwînò* 'we are well'

A rising tone (ˇ) in that position would indicate that the sentence is unfinished, that the completion has to be expected.

e.g.   *tìlì bwìnò, kàyà înu?* 'we are well, and you?'

Questions with interrogatives may have a downgliding tone on the first syllable of the interrogative,

e.g.   *mtèngò wácè bwânji?* 'its price (is) what?'

Affixation can also change the lexical tone of the parts which are in the sequence, e.g. the pronominal prefixes of the verb roots, in subject or object position, occur with low tone or high tone, but the tense/aspect markers appear to be stable, and the pronominals have a fixed tone with them,

e.g.   *-ná --dzá* and *-ká-* have low tone pronouns; so have *-à-* and *kù-* but *-mà-* has high tone ones.

e.g.   *Ndìná bwélà dzùlò*   'I came yesterday'

          Tìná khàlà kùnò   'We live here'

          Mùdzà pìtà kù Lusàkà   'You will go to Lusaka'

          Aàgònà bwìnò   'He slept well'

Ndímàkhálá kùnò	'I live here'
Mmàkhálá kùtí?	'Where do you live?'
Mùngàndíùzè njìlà	'You can tell mc the way'
Àngàtígúlìtsà nyàmà	'He can sell us meat'
Àtìùzè	'He might tell us'

Most of the tone examples above are taken from *ChiNvanja Basic Course* of the Foreign Service Institute, Washington D.C. and from *A Grammar of chiChewa* by M.H. Watkins. The notes in the books frequently indicate discrepancies between the expected and the realised tonal patterns, and differences between Nyanja speakers from different districts. What Watkins wrote in 1973 is still unfortunately true: 'This variation of pitch-accent, resulting in part from the juxtaposition of different patterns, is a complex problem which at present has not been sufficiently analysed and therefore cannot be presented fully in this study.' (Watkins, p. 17).

Chapter II

MORPHOLOGY

Nyanja sentences can be distinguished in a speakers discourse by their intonation patterns. The sentence has an intonation pattern which indicates the end, the point where a speaker may stop expecting to he interrupted, questioned, etc. or go to another point in his or her communication. The smallest unit to form a sentence is a word. For convenience the accepted word division of Cinyanja orthography is used without discussion in this outline. One-word sentences, which show several words in the English translation, are common, e.g.   *Cábwìnò*   'It-is-all-right'

        Mùnákwátìwá?   'Are-you-married?'

        Tìkùkázígúlìtsà   'We-are-going-to-sell-them'

"One-word" sentences like these may also occur as parts of longer sentences,

e.g.   *íkúvúmba*   'it-is-raining' as a predicate of the first clause of:

        Ngàkhálè mvúlà íkùvúmbà

        even-when the rain it-is-raining

        ànthú àwà ámàpítà kù mùndá wángá

        people these they-go to-the- garden-my

        ndí kùmá límá bàsì

        and hoe really

meaning 'even when it rains these people go to my garden and work hard'.

GRAMMATICAL AGREEMENT

The core of the second clause of the long sentence above is the clause:

   anthu awa amapita kumunda wanga 'they go to my garden'.

It consists of the subject nominal phrase *anthu awa* 'these people' and the predicate verbal phrase *amapita kumunda wanga* 'they go to my garden'.

The noun which is the head of the subject nominal phrase *anthu* 'people' governs the following demonstrative *awa* 'these' and the verbal predicate with the subject prefix *a-mapita*. This grammatical agreement or concord is a general characteristic of Bantu languages. All noun modifiers i.e. adjectives, demonstratives, numerals, possessives, locative and relative classes, must agree (i.e. show the concord) with the head noun, and the predicates, verbs, adjectives, and numbers, also agree with the subject noun.

NOUNS

The simplest nouns of Cinyanja consist of stems which have no prefixes in the singular but which have prefixes in the plural:

e.g. *dzombe,* singular, *ma-dzombe,* plural, 'grasshopper',

fuko, singular, *ma-fuko,* plural, 'tribe'.

These prefixes mark the classes to which a noun belongs in the singular and the plural. In many cases singular and plural classes are paired, e.g. classes 1 and 2, 3 and 4, 12 and 13, but others are not, e.g. the plural class 6 with the prefix *ma-* is used for several classes of singulars and seems to be favoured by speakers who use Cinyanja as a second language.

Reduplications of parts of the whole stem are common,

e.g. *m-titima* 'antelope bull'; *n-sasa* 'seeds of cotton'; *nyenyezi* 'star'.

Note that a prefix of the same shape will be found belonging to different classes,

e.g. **mu-** to 1,3 and 18;

ku- to 15 and 17

zi- to 8 and 10 (see Table III)

Most nouns have both a singular and a plural class prefix. But the nouns of class 1a have no class prefix. Note that *ka, na-* and *tsa-,* which occur as first syllables of nouns of this class, are not class prefixes but part of the composite noun,

e.g. *tsa-ka-m-dzi* 'headman of a village',

na-m-kulunga 'a painted basket.'

However the classes 12, singular, and 14, plural, include diminutives which show the normal class prefix after the diminutive prefix

e.g. *ny-ama* 'animal(s)', singular and plural; *ka-ny-ama,* 'a small animal',

10

singular; *ti-ny-ama* 'small animals', plural.

Similarly; *mw-ana* singular, 'child', *a-ana,* plural, 'children', *ka-mw-ana,* singular; 'a baby'.

NOUN CLASSES AND THEIR PREFIXES

Table III

Class	sg./pl.	Prefix	Examples
1	sg.	*mu-, mw-, m- ŋ-*	**mu***-nthu* or *m-nthu* 'person'
			mw*-ana* 'a child'
			m*-kazi* or *ŋ-kazi* 'a woman'
1a	sg.	zero	*garu* 'dog'
			nadzikambe 'chameleon'
2	pl.	*a-*	**a***-nthu* 'persons'
			a*-garu* 'dogs'
			a*-nadzikambe* 'chameleons'
3	sg.	*mu, m-, mw-*	**mu***-dzi* 'village'
4	pl.	*mi-, my-*	**mi***-dzi* 'villages'
5	sg.	*li-, di-, dzi-, -l-*	
		d-, lu-, zero	**li***-mdimi* 'orange'
6	pl.	*ma-*	**ma***-ndimi* 'oranges'
7	sg.	*chi-, ch-*	**chi***-nthu* 'thing'
8	pl.	*zi-, dzi-, dz-, c+vi-*	**zi***-nthu* 'things'
			C+vi-nthu ('things')
9	sg.	*n-, m-, ny-, n-*	**ny***-umba* 'house'
10	pl.	same as above and	

		zi- (rare)	**ny**-*umba* or
			zi-*ny*-*umba* 'houses'
11	nil.	integrated into class 5	
12	sg.	*ka-*	*ka-njira* 'small path'
13	pl.	*ti-*	*ti-njira* 'little paths'
14	sg.	*u-, bu-*	*ukulu(bu-)* 'greatness'
15	sg.	*ku-*	*ku-sauke* 'suffering'
16	sg. + pl.	*pa-*	*pa-khomo* 'at the door'
17	" "	*ku-*	*kuhimbi* 'to, from phimbi'
18	" "	*mu-, m-*	*mumidzi* or *mmidzi* 'in the villages'

Class 1

This class contains living beings, i.e. humans and animals as well as nominalisations of verbs,

e.g.   *m-dindo* 'a watcher' from *ku-linda* 'to watch'

   m-dziwa 'one who knows' from *ku-dziwa* 'to know'

Class 1a

This subsidiary class differs from class 1 in that it has no visible (or surface) class prefix but governs the same syntactic concordance as that imposed by members of class 1. Class 1a is, therefore, said to have a zero prefix.

It contains terms for people, e.g. *nkamwini* 'son-in-law',

for animals e.g. *gogo* 'goat/sheep', and *kavalo* 'horse' (from Portuguese) *cavallo* as well as for things of foreign origin, e.g. *ka-lata* (from *carta*) 'letter';

12

tupa (from Kabanga) 'file'.

Class 2

The plural forms of class 1 regularly fall into this class. The plural of politeness is used when addressing or speaking of adult persons with terms like 'father', 'mother', 'teacher'

e.g.   *a-mai* 'my mother' or *a-zi -mai* 'our mothers'.

Nouns of class 1a have the same class prefix as class 1 prefixed to their stem,

e.g.   *a-garu* 'dogs'   *a-mbiri* 'headmen';

a-mbidzi 'zebras'   *a-kalata* 'letters'

a-tupa 'files'   *a-tsacipala* 'smiths'

Class 3

This class typically contains names of trees, plants, things made from wood, a few animal names as well as some liquids and mass nouns

e.g.   *m-tengo* 'tree'   *mu-nda* 'garden'

mu-dzi 'village'   *m-pando* 'stool'

m-kaka 'milk'   *m-kango* 'lion'

m-chele 'salt'   *mw-endo* 'leg'

Class 4

The plural forms of class 3 fall in this class

e.g.   *mi-tengo* 'trees'   *mi-nda* 'gardens'

mi-dzi 'villages'   *mi-pando* 'stools'

mi-kango 'lions'   *my-endo* 'legs'

13

Class 5

Names for fruit,

e.g.   *li-ula* 'fruit of the *muula* tree'   *duwa* 'flower'

       dzembe 'watermelon'

animals

e.g.   *li-nthumbu* 'red ant'

and parts of the body,

e.g.   *dzi-no* 'tooth'   *di-so* 'eye'

       thupi 'body'   *pfupa* 'bone'

       phandu 'front tooth'

as well as nominalisations are frequently found in this class

e.g.   *li-kulu* 'greatness'   *dindilo* 'watchtower' (*kulindira* 'to watch')

Nouns like

       khasu 'hoe'   *dzi-ko* 'earth'

also belong to this class.

Cl. 5 is also used for indicating time

e.g.   *li-ti* 'when'   *dzulo li--ja* 'that day long ago'

Nouns with the prefix *lu,*

e.g.   *lu-panga* 'knife, sword'   *lu-pya* 'burnt bush' (*ku-psya* 'to burn')

       lu-lime 'tongue

do not have a class of their own, as in other Bantu languages, but govern the concordance *li-,*

e.g.   *lu-panga li-kulu* 'a big knife'

Class 6

This class contains the plural forms of class 5 and some of class 14. The plural prefix *ma-* in most cases replaces the singular prefixes *li-* or *di-,* e.g.   *ma-ula* 'fruits of the *muula* tree'

  ma-nthumba 'red ants'

  ma-no 'teeth'   *ma-so* 'eyes'

In others *ma-* is prefixed to the singular noun,

e.g.   *ma-dindilo* 'watchtowers'

Ma-dziko 'earth' is used as well as *ma-ko* and *ma-iko* in different dialects.

The plural forms of class 14 show the *ma-* prefix before the *u-* prefix of the singular

e.g.   *ma-u-dzu* 'grasses'   *ma-u-kulu* 'fleas'

  ma-u-dziwa 'knowledge'

Nouns which have no prefix in the singular often have a stem in the plural which has a fricative without the initial stop of the affricate form found in the singular,

e.g.   *ma-fupa* 'bones' from the singular *pfupa*

  ma-siku 'days' from the singular *tsiku*

Other stems occur without the aspiration of the initial stop

e.g.   *ma-pandu* 'front teeth' (sing. *phandu*)

  ma-tupi 'bodies' (sing. *thupi*)

  ma-kasu 'hoes' (sing. *khasu*)

Nominalisations of verbs are common in this class, often indicating the manner or the reason for an action

e.g.   *ma-cokero* 'going, manner of going, reason for going away'

  (*ku-cokera* 'to go away')

  ma-pephero 'asking, means of begging, excuse for asking' (*ku-pempha* 'beg')

15

Class 7

This class is often called the 'class for things' including nouns like

e.g. *chi-ntu* 'thing'   *chi-panda* 'wooden spoon'

     cha-bvi 'fishnet'

The 'thing' class also includes a number of abstracts

e.g. *chi-soni* 'compassion'   *chi-bwenzi* 'friendship'

     chi-lungamo 'justice'

Nouns of other classes which are put into class 7 acquire an augmentative and often also derogatory meaning

e.g. *chi-njira* 'a broad road'   *chi-tsamba* 'a large leaf'

     chi-ntenda 'great sickness'   *chi-mwana* 'a big child'

     chi-dzete 'a fool'   *chi-wanda* 'an evil spirit'

Class 8

The variations of the prefix *zi-*, *dz-*, for plurals of class 7 seem to be dialectical forms

e.g. *dz-aka* or *z-aka* 'years' (sing. *chaka*)

     dz-ala 'fingers' (sing. *ch-ala*)

     dzi-manga or *zi-manga* 'maize', (sing. *chi-manga*)

Cichewa (Cinyanja) has two prefix forms, viz. the usual *vi-* alternates with *zi-*, but involving a slight difference in meaning

e.g. *chi-nthu* 'a thing', *vi-nthu* 'things' and *zi-nthu* 'things in general' that is, things not definitely conceived (Watkins). In the Lilongwe District *dzi-nthu* is used for 'crops, foodstuffs'.

Class 9

This class is sometimes called the animal class. It contains many animal names e.g. *n-chefu* 'eland'   *n-galu* 'crested crane'

n-goma 'kudu'   *n-jobvu* 'elephant'

It also contains titles of human dignitaries

e.g. *m-fumu* 'chief'   *mbiri* 'headman', (also class 1)

m-fulu 'free man'

tools, and other objects

e.g. *ŋ-oma* 'drum'   *ny-ale* 'lamp, light'

ny-umba 'house'

and nominalizations of verbs and adjectives

e.g. *ny-imbo* 'song'   *n-chito* 'work'

m-fupi 'nearness'

Class 10

Most of the plurals of nouns in (singular) class 9 have the same shape in the singular and plural form. The difference in number shows up in the concord prefix (see Table IV),

e.g. *ny-ama i-modzi* 'one animal'; *ny-ama zi-tatu* 'three animals'

A few nouns show the plural with a prefix

e.g. *zi-mfulu* 'free men', (sing. *mfulu*); *zi-nyao* 'drawings' (sing. *nyao*)

Class 11 of neighbouring Bantu languages is integrated into class 5 in Cinyanja.

Class 12

This class consists of diminutives derived from nouns of other classes. The prefix of class 12 (*ka-*) is either found in the prefix slot or is put before the original class prefix

e.g. *ka-nthu* 'a small thing' (compare with *chi-nthu* 'a thing')

17

ka-mw-ana 'an infant', *ka-ny-ama* 'a little beast' (see page 10 above).

Class 13

The plurals of class 12 follow the same pattern as that described for the singular class 12

e.g.   *ti-nthu* 'small things' *ti-mi-tengo* 'little trees'

The dialect of the Dedza District uses the prefix *tu-*,

e.g.   *tu-n-tondo* 'small mortars'

This variation is locally ascribed to the influence of the Ngoni people who settled there.

Class 14

A small number of nouns, most of which are abstracts, as well as derivations from verbs, adjectives and nouns of other classes are to be found in this class,

e.g.   *u-cenjera* 'cleverness', (from *kucenjera* 'to be clever')

u-tali 'distance, length', (from *tali* 'far, long')

ubw-ana 'childhood', (*mw-ana* class 1).

Some are mass nouns

e.g.   *u-ci*, 'honey'   *u-fa* 'flour'

Only a few of the nouns of this class have plurals, usually in class 5

e.g.   *u-ta* 'ball', plural *ma-uta*

u-siku 'night', pl. *ma-u-siku*

bw-ato 'canoe', pl. *ma-bw-ato*

Class 15

Most of the nouns in this class are infinitive-nominals

e.g.   *ku-yera* 'to be white = light'

ku-ipa 'to be bad = evil'

ku-imba 'to sing = singing'

Classes 16/17/18

Classes 16/17/18 are grammatically classified as 'locative' classes. The prefixes are like prepositions of place or direction,

viz.   *pa-* 'at, on'

       ku- 'in the area, the direction of'

and   *mu-* 'in'

e.g.   *pa-n-si* 'on the ground'   *ku-mu-dzi* 'to, from the village'

       mu-ny-umba 'in the house'

The grammatical syntactic concordance or agreement shows that these locative nouns form a special class and are not a preposition followed by a noun (as in Indo-European languages). The locative prefix governs the modifiers and the predicate in the same way as any other noun class prefix (see page 9).

e.g.   **ku**-*mudzi* **ku**-*li* **ku**-*fupi* '(to) the village it is near = the village is near'

MODIFIERS OF NOUNS AND THEIR CONCORDS

The agreement between the head noun, the modifiers and the predicate is shown by concord prefixes, identical with or related to the noun class prefix.

In class 1 and 18, the nasal *m-* of the prefix occurs also in the secondary form of the prefix (see Table IV).

Classes 3, 4 6, 9 and 10 have secondary concord prefixes without the nasals of the primary forms. The tertiary forms consist of the secondary with the suffix -*a* (cf. Table IV). The use of the different forms is related to the word-classes as shown in the following paragraphs regarding numerals, adjectives and demonstratives.

Table IV

Noun Agreement Prefixes

Class	Primary Forms	Secondary Forms	Tertiary Forms
1.	*mu-*	*m-, mu-, u-*	*wa*
1a.	*none*	*mu-, u-*	*wa-*
2.	*a-(C: va-)*	*a-(C: va)*	*aa- + (vaa-)*
3.	*mu-*	*u-*	*wa-*
4.	*mi-*	*i-*	*ya-*
5.	*li-, dzi-, lu-*	*li-, i-*	*la-*
6.	*ma-*	*a-(C: va-)*	*aa- + (vaa-)*
7.	*chi-*	*chi-, ch-*	*cha-*
8.	*zi-(C: vi-)*	*zi-(C: vi-)*	*za-(C: vaa)*
9.	*n-*	*i-*	*ya-*
10.	*n-*	*zi-, z-*	*za-*
11.	*ka-*	*ka-, k-*	*ka-*
12.	*ti-, tu-*	*ti-, t-, tu-*	*ta-, twa*
13.	*u-, ubw-*	*u-, bu-*	*wa-, bwa-*
14.	*ku-*	*ku-*	*kwa-*
15.	*pa-*	*pa-*	*pa-*
16.	*ku-*	*ku-*	*kwa-*
17.	*mu-*	*mu-*	*mwa-*

Numerals

The simplest examples of the concord system can be seen in noun phrases which have a numeral modifying the head noun. The stems of numbers one to

20

five are: *-modzi* 'one', *-wiri* 'two', *-tatu* 'three', *-nai* 'four', *-sanu* 'five'. These take secondary form (cf. Table IV) of the class prefix of the noun they modify, e.g.

1.	*m-nthu*	**m**-*modzi*	'one person'
1a.	*garu*	**m**-*modzi*	'one dog'
2.	*a-kazi*	**a**-*wiri*	'two women'
3.	*mw-endo*	**u**-*modzi*	'one leg'
4.	*mi-dzi*	**i**-*tatu*	'three villages'
5.	*dzi-no*	**li**-*modzi*	'one tooth'
6.	*ma-no*	**a**-*nai*	'four teeth'
7.	*chi-nthu*	**chi**-*modzi*	'one thing'
8.	*z-aka*	**zi**-*sanu*	'five years'

A similar pattern applies in all classes which have count nouns. Numbers higher than five are usually borrowed from English. This applies sometimes even in the case of small numbers

e.g. *sikisi* 'six'

Quantifiers and Intensifiers

Some modifiers with meaning like 'some', 'all', 'much', 'many', 'each', 'every', 'few', 'other', etc. behave like numerals and take the secondary concord

e.g. *dzuwa **l**-onse* 'all day'

*ufa **w**-ambiri* 'much flour'

*zi-nthu **z**-ambiri* 'many things'

With the nouns of class 1 they take *u-*

e.g. *mu-nthu **w**-ina (**u**-ina)* 'another person', where (**u**- before *-i, -e, -a*

21

becomes *w-*; see page 20).

Adjectives

Adjectives proper are a small class of words in Cinyanja. Many adjectival meanings are instead expressed by verbs like, 'be clever'; be red, white, dark'; 'be lucky'. Adjectives take both the tertiary concord followed by the secondary in that order:

Class 1.	*mw-ana*	**wa-m-ŋono**	'a small child'
2.	*a-kazi*	**a-a-tali**	'tall women'
3.	*m-tengo*	**wa-u-kulu**	'a tall tree'
4.	*mitengo*	**ya-i-kulu**	'tall trees'
5.	*khasu*	**la-li-fupi**	'short hoes'
6.	*ma-kasu*	**a-a-fupi**	'short hoes'
7.	*chi-pewa*	**cha-chi-ŋono**	'a small hat'
8.	*zi-pewa*	**ʐa-ʐi-kulu**	'small hats'
16.	*pa-khomo*	**pa-pa-kulu**	'at the big door'
17.	*ku-sukulu*	**kwa-ku-tali**	'to the faraway school'
18.	*mu-ny-umba*	**mwa-mu-kulu**	'in the big house'

Demonstratives

These indicate distance, i.e. proximity to or remoteness from the speaker or hearer or both and are in some cases a variation of the secondary concord prefix. In other words, they are similar to adjectives.

i) The simplest form of 'this' and 'these' has the shape of the secondary concord with the vowel of the concord as initial syllable,

   e.g.   *ili, ici, umu, aka, apa*

22

Concords which consist of a single vowel add a glide between the repetition, -*w*- or -*y*-

Class 1.   *uyu* 'this'

2.   *awa* 'these'

3.   *uwu* 'this'

4.   *iyi* 'these'

5.   *ili* 'this'

6.   *awa* 'these'

7.   *ichi* 'this'

8.   *izi* 'these'

9.   *iyi* 'this'

10.   *izi* 'these'

11.   *aka* 'this'

12.   *aka* 'this'

13.   *iti* 'these'

14.   *uwu* 'this'

15.   *uku* 'this'

16.   *apa* 'this here'

17.   *uku* 'to, from this'

18.   *umu* 'in here'

These demonstratives can also occur bound to the noun they modify; they have or show no initial vowel and arc suffixed, i.e. occur as suffixes:

e.g. *mwanayu* (*mwana-yu*) 'this child'

      tinthuti (*tinthu-ti*) 'these little things'

ii)   A more distant 'that' is expressed by demonstratives which have a final -*o* replacing the vowel of the concord. These occur in both free and bound forms

e.g. *mkazi uyo* or *mkaziyo* 'that woman'

The most remote 'that, far away' is of an adjectival shape, *-ja,* and uses the secondary concords

e.g. *a-nthu **a-ja*** 'those people over there'

It is also used for 'those I mentioned before, you know who I mean'.

iii) A similar type, ***-no*** 'this very thing', expresses an emphasis. It is frequently used for time and location but rarely in other noun classes,

e.g. *tsiku li-**no*** 'this very day'

 c-aka (*ci-aka*) *ci-**no*** 'this present year'

 *pa-ansi pa-**no*** 'just here below'

Pronouns

Cinyanja has sets of pronouns for nouns of all classes. Their distribution is syntatically determined (see page 33).

Free forms can occur like nouns, e.g. in answer to a question like: 'Who (or what) is this/are these?'

Ndani aliko? 'Who is there?' ***Ine****.* 'It is I.'

The free forms of the personal pronouns are:

ine 'I, me'	*ife* 'we, us'
iwe 'thou, thee' ('you' singular)	*inu* 'you' (plural, or respectful)
iye 'he, she, him, her'	*iwo* 'they, them'

The other noun classes (i.e. other than those served by the personal pronouns as illustrated above) use forms similar to the secondary forms of demonstratives with the initial *i-* similar to the personal pronouns above:

Class	3.	*iwo* 'it'	4.	*izo* 'they, them'
	5.	*ilo* 'it'	6.	*iwo* 'they, them'
	7.	*icho* 'it'	8.	*izo* 'they, them'

Nouns Modified by Nouns

In noun phrases of this type the tertiary concord of the head noun is prefixed to the modifier,

e.g.   *zi-patso za-mitengo*   'fruits of trees'

        pa-kati pa-madzi   'in the middle of the water'

If the modifier noun is locative, e.g. the place of origin, the same pattern is found:

e.g.   *nsomba za-mu-ny-anja*   'fish-of-in the lake = lake fish'

Nouns Modified by Verbal Nominals

Verbs of one syllable used as modifiers show the infinitive prefixed by the tertiary concord of the head noun,

e.g.   *nsaru ya-ku-da*   'cloth of being black = black cloth'

        Chimanga cha-ku-psya   'maize of being ripe = ripe maize'

Verb stems of two or more syllables used as modifiers are prefixed by contracted forms of the tertiary concord of the head noun followed by a variant of the infinitive prefix,

e.g.   *thuùpì l-óò-cépà*   'a body which is small = a small body'

                                   instead of *thù-pì lá-kù-cé-pà*

        ùfà w-óò-yèlà   'flour which is white = white flour'

                                     instead of *u-fa wa-ku-yela*

The -*k*- of the infinitive prefix is dropped and the resulting fusion -*u*- consists of a long -*oo*- with a falling tone.

Nouns Modified by Relative Clauses

Where a free relative pronoun is required for emphasis or for syntactical reasons the stem -*mene* 'same' is used with the secondary prefix except in class 1 which has -*a*,

e.g. **tinaona mwana** *amene anagulitsa mkaka*   'we saw a child who was selling milk.'

     Mkaka **umene** *tinagula uli kuti?*   'Where is the milk which we bought?'

VERBS

As indicated on pages 8-9 a Nyanja sentence may consist of one verbal word like *tikukazigulitsa* 'we are going round to sell them.' Forms like these consist of a subject prefix

    ti-

tense prefix

        -ku-

aspect 'intention' prefix

           -ka-

object infix

              -zi-

verb root

                  (n) gul-

causative extension

                     -its-

verb final suffix

                       -a

Verb Roots

A verb root is that part of a verbal word which remains when all affixes have been separated. Verb roots are of different shapes:

i)   **C (Consonant)**

  The simplest verb root consists of a single consonant

e.g. *-b-* 'steal'; *-c-* 'dawn' *-kh-* 'drop'; *-dz-* 'come'; *-ph-* 'kill'

ii) **C (Consonant) + W or Y**

  Some roots consist of a consonant followed by an approximant, (or semi-vowel)

e.g. *-dy-* 'eat'; *mw-* 'drink'; *-gw-* 'fall'; *-phw-* 'dry/up'

iii) **CVC (Consonant, Vowel, Consonant)**

  The most common shape consists of a consonant followed by a vowel and a second consonant

e.g. *-kul-* 'grow'; *-nen-* 'speak'; *-pim-* 'measure'; ***-los-*** 'predict'

Note that when the consonant is an aspirated stop or an affricate, it is symbolized by (or written with) two letters (or graphemes) to represent one sound. This tends to confuse the shape of the CVC pattern in writing,

e.g. *-khal-* 'sit'; *-pfik-* 'itch'; *-tsal-* 'remain'; *-tsats-* 'barter' where ***kh, pf***
and ***ts*** represent one sound but symbolised by two letters.

Dialect versions of the affricates as fricatives are also found (see page 6 above).

The second consonant of the CVC pattern frequently occurs nasalized,

e.g. *-demb-* 'be white'; *-fung-* 'lock'; *-funkh-* 'remove'

  -pemph- 'ask, pray'; *-land-* 'steal'; *-panth-* 'hammer, beat'

  -funds- 'ask'; *-punz-* 'learn'

iv) Roots which start with a vowel often have an approximant *-w* or *-y* added when preceded by a prefix which ends in a vowel,

e.g.   *-amb-* or *-yamb-* 'begin'

           -er- or *-yer-* 'be white'

           -on- or *-won-* 'see'

           -imb- or *-yimb-* 'sing'

v) Roots of more than one syllable frequently show a reduplication of the following shapes: Consonant 1, Vowel 1, Consonant 1, Vowel 1, Consonant 2

e.g.   *-bebed-* 'nibble'; *-dodom-* 'doubt'

           -fufum- 'swell'; *-kikut-* or *-kukukut-* 'eat something hard'

           also, with prenasalised CI:

e.g.   *-ndandal-* 'go to-and-fro'; *njonjol-* 'run fast'

Others show a consonant vowel, Consonant 1, Vowel 1, Consonant 2, Vowel 1, Consonant 3,

e.g.   *-tambalal-* 'stretch out'; *-tsokomol-* 'cough'; *-phudzumuk-* 'escape'

Verb Final Suffixes: are *-a* and *-e*

One of these is obligatory for every verbal word except for the defective (i.e. exceptional) verbs

e.g.   *ku-li* 'to be' and *ku-ti* 'to say'

Final - *a* occurs in all infinitive verbal forms with the exception of the defective verbs indicated above,

e.g.   *kulir-**a*** 'to cry'; *kudzandion-**a*** 'to come - and-see-me'

28

Most tense/aspect markers co-occur with final -*a*. This will be discussed in Verb Extensions on page 30.

Final -*e* occurs in verbal forms:

a) used as polite requests, permissions and refusals,

e.g. *tipite* 'let's go'; *katenge madzi* 'go and draw water'

   mubwele 'please come back'; *musalowe* 'don't enter'

b) with the markers *si-......-na-* 'not yet'

e.g. *sindinalimwe* 'I-have-not-yet-heard-it' (see below page 34).

c) with the marker -*nga*- 'can'

e.g. *ndingakwele basi* 'I-can-take a bus' (See below page 35).

d) independent clauses,

e.g. *Akufuna kuti tikhale pano.* 'He wants that we should sit here, i.e. he wants us to sit here.'

Post Final Verbal Suffixes

These occur in various forms:

a) -*ni* indicates the plural in the imperatives,

e.g. *ima-ni* (you, plural or respect 'stand')

b) -*thu* and -*di* stress the meaning of the verb-root.

e.g. *mukucidziwa-thu* 'you know it really well'; *ndithu-di* 'it is indeed'

c) as locative (enclitic) suffices -*po*, -*ko*, -*mo,* related to the noun classes 16, 17, 18,

e.g. *anagona-po* 'they-slept-at-that-place'

   mubwela-ko liti 'when do-you-return there?'

   Nkhuku zili-mo 'the chickens are-in-there'

Verb Extensions are infixed after the verb-root before the final *-a* or *-e*. They imply variations of the basic meaning,

e.g. *bwela* 'return' ***bwelela*** 'return to or from'

    bweza 'bring back' ***bweleza*** 'do something again' ***bwezela*** 'return, repay'

However, some verbs which appear to have the shape of an extended verb form do not occur in a simple or unextended form, i.e. the simple root is not used,

e.g. ***nunudzila*** 'eat little by little'

There are at least seven, probably more, extension infixes, but they do not occur with every verb-root. In many cases two or three extensions are co-occurrent.

The extension is linked to the verb root by a vowel in harmony with the last vowel of the root, i.e. *-i* after *-a-, -i-, -u-,*

e.g. *kalamba* 'grow old'   *kalamb-**itsa*** 'grow very old'

    pinda 'fold'   *pindi-ki-**ila*** 'hook'

    khula 'rub'   *khul-**ila*** 'rub smooth'

but *-e-* after *-e-* and *-o-,*

    nena 'speak'   *nen-**eza*** 'inform'

    pota 'spin'   *pot-**eza*** 'twist around'

The specific shapes of verb extensions are more easily described than the semantic relations between simple and extended verb roots and the general range of meaning of the extensions. The labels given to the following extensions are therefore only an approximation (see Table V).

a) **Applicative extension *-il/-el-*:**

e.g.   *anaphika nsima* 'She cooked maize porridge'

*ana-ndi-**phik-ila** nsima* 'She cooked maize porridge for me'

capa 'wash clothes'; ***pocap-il-a*** 'a place far washing cloth, i.e. laundry'

tsegula 'open'; ***tsegul-ikil-a*** *nkhuku* 'Let the fowls out e.g. open for the fowls'

nena 'speak'; *andi**nen-el-a*** 'they speak for me'

b) **Stative extension *-ik-/-ek-*:**

e.g.   *taya* 'lose, throw away'; *nda**tay-ik-a*** 'I have lost my way'

ona 'look'; *mwezi wa**on-ek-a-*** 'the moon is visible'

c) **Associative/reciprocal extension *-an-***

e.g.   *nena* 'speak'; ***anen-an-a*** 'they speak together'

leka 'stop'; *tika**lek-an-a*** *pati* 'where do we part'

d) **Passive extension *-w-*:**

This is rarely used, active forms being preferred, e.g. 'somebody stole the cattle' instead of 'the cattle were stolen.'

The passive extension occurs often as *-dw-*, probably a fusion of the applicative *-i-* with the passive *-w-*. Verb roots which end in *-i-* also have *-d-* before *-w-*.

e.g.   *bala* 'bear'; ***bad-w-a*** 'be born'

gula 'buy'; ***gud-w-a*** 'be bought'

panda 'trample'; ***pond-ed-w-a*** 'be trodden on'

d) **Causative extensions**

These are of various shapes.

i) The simplest is *-y-* which occurs after nasals,

e.g.   *lema* 'be tired'; *ati**lem-y-a*** 'they weary us'

        komana 'meet'; ***koman-ya-*** 'bring people together'

ii) Non-nasal consonants are changed: *k + y* becomes ***ts***,

e.g.   *leka* 'stop'; *usandi-**leitse*** 'don't stop me'

        oneka 'be visible'; *anazi-**onetsa** ŋombe zonse* 'He exhibited all the cattle'

iii) *p + y* becomes *ps* or ***psy***

e.g.   *lipa* 'pay for a case'; ***lipsa*** 'take revenge'

        cepa 'be small'; *a-**cepesya** mtengo* 's/he has made the price small' i.e. 's/he has lowered the price'

iv) *l + y* becomes *z*

e.g.   *lila* 'cry'; *ana-**liza** madzi* (literally 's/he has made the water cry'): 's/he splashed the water'

v) *nd+y* or *ng +y* becomes ***nz***

e.g.   *tanda* 'extend'; ***tanza** dzanja* 'stretch the hand out'

        donga 'arrange'; *ali wo**donza*** 'she is careful'

Many verbal words with a causative extension have an intensive meaning

e.g.   *bvomela* 'answer'; ***bvomel-ez-a*** 'respond in chorus'

        pha 'kill'; *wa**ph-its-a*** 'you killed very much'

(f) **Reverse extension *-ul-***

e.g.   *yala* 'spread out'; ***kayal-ul-e** mphasa zanu* 'go and roll up your mats'

        pfunda 'wrap'; *njoka zi**pfund-ul-a*** 'snakes cast off their skins'

g) Extension by reduplication of the full verb stem

This implies repetition distribution

e.g.   *thonje la-**mangana-mangana*** 'the thread is wound round and round'

        *a-**khuula-khuula*** *mpongwe zao* 'He polishes his axe handles all over'

VERB PREFIXES

Verb prefixes are markers of concords, tense, aspect, and the negative. Their order is fixed as listed in the following description:

Initial Prefixes

The initial prefixes of a verbal word forming the predicate of a sentence is in most cases a pronominal affix governed by the previously expressed or the implied subject of the sentence i.e. it is either personal or concordial:

e.g. ***ndi**nagula nsomba* 'I bought fish'

     Nsomba zi zi nabvunda 'these fish are bad'

'Bound' pronouns occur affixed to the verb in the subject or in the object position;

e.g. ***ndi-ku**-ona* 'I-you- see', (subject-object-verb)

Personal pronouns have the following bound forms:

Subject	Object
ndi-, nd- 'I'	***ndi-*** 'me'
u-, w- 'you' (sg.)	***-ku-*** 'you' (sg.)
a- 'he, she'	***-mu-, -m-*** 'him, her'
ti-, t- 'we'	***-ti-*** 'us'
mu-, mw- 'you' (pl.)	***-ku-*** (stem) ***-ni-*** 'you' (pl.)
a- 'they'	***-wa-*** 'them'

33

The pronoun prefixes **ndi-** and **ti-** occur without the vowel **-i-** in the subject position before -*a*-,

e.g.   *ndine* **nd**-*a-dza* 'it is me, I have come'

   ife **t**-*a-dya* 'we, we have already eaten'

   ndine **nd**-*oona* (*nd-aona*) 'I saw (it) myself'

U-, mu- occur as **w-, mw-** in subject or object position before **-a-**,

e.g.   **w**-*a-fika* 'you arrived' (sing.) (*u-a-fika*)

   mw-a-fika 'you arrived' (pl.) (*mu-afika*)

   mw-ankha 'answer him' (*mu-a-nkha*)

This last example has the alternative form **mu-y-ankha**. The same glide is frequently heard at the beginning of verb roots of the VC pattern,

e.g.   **mu-y**-*angata,* (also **mu-w**-*angata*) 'carry him'

The Noun Classes

These use the secondary form of concord in both subject and object positions

e.g.   *Chimangachi,* **chi***bvunda.   Tina***chi***gula kuChibwe.* 'Maize-this it-is rotten. We-it-bought from-Chibwe'.

   Nkuku **zi***bwera muminda. Ndidza***zi***pha.* 'Chickens-they-come into-the gardens. I shall them-kill'.

The concord in the object position occasionally refers to a following, not previously mentioned, noun,

e.g.   *Kodi njokayi itha ku-**wa**-pha a-nthu* 'Can this snake kill people?'

The Negative Markers *s-, si-, sa-*

These occur in various places of the verbal construction but always before the verb root:

si- occurs as first prefix before the pronominal or concordial prefixes in verbal

34

words which have final -*a*- and the "defective" verb roots -*li* and *ti-;*

e.g.   *Dzuwa si-lilikuwala* 'The sun is not shining'

   Si-muli ndi ana (gloss 'you are not with children'), meaning 'You do not have children'

   Si-muti kantu 'You do not say anything'

s- occurs before -*u*- 'you' (sg.) and -*a*- 'he',

e.g.   *S'-analowa (si-analowa) m'nyumba* 'he did not enter the house'

Si- co-occurs also with the aspect marker -*nga*- and final -*e* (see page 29).

Tense Signs

In many cases the tense signs set the tonal pattern for the verbal word e.g., after -*ku*-, the verb has high tones:

e.g.   *mùkùpítá* 'you are going'   *mùkùcókélá* 'you are coming'

but after -*na*- low tones follow:

e.g.   *mùnápìtà* 'you went'   *mùnácòkèlà* 'you came'

-*a*-   occurs with the connotation of past events which persist in the present, indicating a state,

e.g.   *khasi l-a-tyoka* 'the hoe is broken'

   mw-a-dwala 'you are ill (and still are)'

Note that *w*-, not *a*-, co-occurs with the tense markers -*a*- as subject prefix of class 1,

e.g.   *mwana w-a-gona* 'the child fell asleep (and has not yet woken up)'

The tense marker -*a*- is frequently used in narration.

-*ma*- implies continuance over a long period, habit or custom,

e.g.   *ti-ma-khala kuno* 'we have always lived here'

*a-**ma**-yankula Cinyanja* 'they speak Cinyanja'

-***na***- refers to past actions which are perfect, i.e. finished

e.g.   *ti-**na**-fika kale* 'we came a long ago'

-***dza***- indicates future,

e.g.   *mu-**dza**-bwela liti* 'when will you come back?'

-***ta***- indicates that the action was completed in the past before another started,

e.g.   *mphuzitsi a-**ta**-coka* 'when the teacher had gone'

   *ti-**ta**-dziwa* 'when we know (that)'

-***nga***- refers to a possibility, a disposition rather than the physical ability. It co-occurs with the verb final suffix -*e*,

e.g.   *ti-**nga**-wathandize* 'we can help them'

   *mu-**nga**-ndi-uze* 'you can tell me'

-***zi*** expresses an obligation, a must

e.g.   *ti-**zi**-pangana* 'we must agree'

In Cichewa the same particle occurs with a future, repeated or habitual action,

e.g.   *ti-**zi**-gula mkaka* 'we will always buy milk'

-***ngo***- occurs with a sense of restriction, minimising the verb,

e.g.   *ti-**ngo**-yenda pansi* 'we are just walking on foot'

-***kà***- occurs only in conditional clauses ('if, when, in case...') with a complementary clause following. It is not found in verbal words with sentence

36

final intonation (see below page 41). In the verbal word, it precedes the tense markers following the pronominal concord,

e.g. *mùkàcòkà pànò sìmùdzá lípìdwà* 'If you leave here (i.e. if you abscond) you will not be paid'

ìkànàfìkà mvúlà tíkànàbzálá címàngà 'If the rains had come, we would have gone to sow maize'

Multiple Tense/Aspect Markers

These occur in some positive and all negative tenses

e.g. *A-na-li-ku yankhula nafe* 'They were talking with us'

Mwezi u-s-a-na-cele 'The moon has not yet risen'

The combination *-li-ku-* occurs as a present progressive tense marker as well as with the past tense marker *-na-*,

e.g. *ti-li-ku-phunzila* 'We are learning'

mu-na-li-ku-bvina 'you were dancing'

These constructions can be regarded alternatively as two verbal words, the first a form of the defective verb stem *-li* 'be' and the second an infinitive, an auxiliary verb construction.

Two directional aspect markers occur usually following tense markers:

-ka- implies 'going' and *-dza-* 'coming'

e.g. *Ndikukagula njinga* 'I am going to buy a bicycle'

ana-dza-tithandiza 'They came and helped us'

Frequently directional markers occur in infinitives,

e.g. *afuna ku-ka-bvinda* 'He wants to go and dance'

ndabwela ku-dza-wona 'I have come to come and see them'

37

ADVERBIAL WORDS

These usually follow the predicate verbal words. They are invariable (that is they do not change) in shape and are governed by concordance. They include ideophones and intensifiers as illustrated below.

Ideophones

Ideophones are restricted to co-occurrence with certain verbal roots. In some cases the shape of the ideophone resembles the corresponding verbal root. Ideophones have special phonemes and structures, such as final consonants, like *gurr*, imitating the sound of pouring flour into a boiling pot.

e.g. *nsomba zingunda **gu! gu!*** 'The fish are knocking (against the fish trap) ***gu gu***'

*ndau-lasa mtengo **mba*** 'I hit the tree ***mba***, i.e., firmly'

*Ulendo undi-lefula **lefu*** 'The journey tires me out'

*kwati-dera **bi** munjira* 'It has become very dark for us on the road'

Intensifiers

These occur almost without restriction. Most frequently used are:

bwino 'well', right'	*Acita **bwino***. 'He has acted well'
kwambili 'much, greatly'	*Awedza nsomba **kwambili*** 'They fish very much'
ndithu 'really, truly'	*Ndabvutika **ndithu*** 'I have had a lot of trouble'

INTERROGATIVES

Words used as question markers or indicators, are either invariable like ***kodi*** or variable nominals like ***-ti, -ngati- -ani, -nji***.

Kodi is often used to indicate a question which may or may not have another interrogative. It occurs at the beginning or at the end of an utterance, e.g.   *Kodi anafika?* 'Did he arrive?' or *Anafika kodi?* 'Did he arrive?'

Variable interrogatives occur with nominal (noun) class prefixes, and in the cases of *ti* and *ngati* with the secondary form as below.

a)   *-ti*

e.g.   *Anafika li-ti?* 'When did he arrive?'

        Acokela ku-ti? 'Where does he come from?'

        Kodi adya zipatso zi-ti? 'Which fruit did they eat?'

        Mwana u-ti akudwala? 'Which child is ill?'

b)   *-ngati* 'how many'

e.g.   *Muli ndi ŋombe zi-ngati?* 'How many cows have you?'

c)   *nji* occurs with the tertiary form of noun class prefix,

e.g.   *Mwagula nyama ya-nji?* 'What kind of meat did you buy?'

        Mwayenda bwa-nji? 'How did you travel?'

        Tizagona munyumba mu-nji? 'In what house shall we sleep?'

d)   *-ani* 'who, whom, what' has the shape *ndani* referring to nouns of classes 1 and 2. This is probably a contraction of *ndi + ani* 'it is who'. It also occurs dialectically as *yani,*

e.g.   *Nd-ani afuna nsomba?* 'Who wants fish?'

        Kodi mwaita nd-ani? 'Whom did you call?'

        Tikauza y-ani? 'Who can we tell?'

In concordance with nouns of class 7, it is prefixed as follows:

        Chi-ani chatyoka? 'What was broken?'

        Chifukwa chi-ani ulila? 'Why do you cry?'

Connectors

These are invariable words or stems used to join nominals or sentences. The

39

most frequent words are:

> *ndi* 'and, with'; *koma* 'but'; *ndipo* 'then'; *apo, pali* 'there';
>
> *ndipo* 'and then'; *ngati* 'if'; *ngakhale* 'even';
>
> *nanga* 'how', and *na-, ni-+*

e.g.　*Atate **ndi** amai anabwela **ndi** mwana* 'The father and the mother came with the child'

　　*Tengani zobvala **ndi** kuzicapa **ndi** kucisa* 'Take the clothes and wash and iron them'

　　*Sitifuna nsomba **koma** nkhuku* 'We do not want fish but chicken'

　　*Tinaziona **koma** zinathawa* 'We saw them but they ran away'

Examples of prefixed connectors

na- with a pronoun or demonstrative:

e.g.　*kodi anayenda **na-nu**?* 'Did he go with you?'

　　*Iai, sanayende **na-fe*** 'No he did not go with-us'

ndi- with a noun phrase or demonstrative

e.g.　*Muli **ndinjinga**?* 'Do you have a bicycle?'

　　*Inde, **ndinayo*** 'Yes. I have one'

ni- connecting two sentences

e.g.　*Nkhuku zibwela kuminda **nizidya** mbeu zatu* 'The chickens come into the gardens and they eat our seeds'

Chapter III

SENTENCES

Nyanja syntax has not yet been fully described. The following is a short outline of the main sentence types. They are here classified as:

a)   non-verbal sentences

b)   uni-verbal sentences, and

c)   multi-verbal sentences.

NON-VERBAL SENTENCES

These are usually short statements of questions and responses which have a sentence or a question intonation pattern (see page 8). The words *ndi* 'it is, they are', or *si* 'it is not, they are not' frequently occur in them.

e.g.   *Chabwino* 'It is all right'

*Atate **ndi** aphunzitsi* 'My father is a teacher'

*kodi lelo **ndi** Lolemba?* 'Is today Monday?'

*Iai, **si** Lolemba, **ndi** Lachiwili* 'No not Monday, it is Tuesday'

UNI-VERBAL SENTENCES

Uni-verbal sentences are the shortest form of sentence comprising one verbal word with or without affixes to the verb stem.

Imperatives and all positive and negative tenses except *-ka-* (see page 37) can occur in univerbal sentences,

e.g.   *bwela* 'come back'

ndidzakuphunzitsani 'I will help you'

Sentences of this type are mainly used in every-day work situations. In formal speech and in writing longer sentences are more common.

A typical pattern of sentence order can be deduced from the following:

> *Pobwela mwana wamkazi anasenza Nthondo paphewa.* 'On returning the girl lifted Nthondo on the shoulder.'

This sentence is made up of the following syntactic elements:

> *pobwela*, a nominal-verbal of class 16 as temporal;
>
> *mwana wamkazi*, a noun modified by a noun as subject;
>
> *anasenza*, a verbal word, as predicate;
>
> *Nthondo*, a noun, as object;
>
> *paphewa*, a noun of cl. 16, as locative. This is represented by the following formula: T+S+V+O+L (i.e. temporal + subject + verb + object + locative).

Words which can be subjects of sentences have been described in the section on nouns.

Objects are of the same word classes as subjects.

The sequence S+V+O occurs frequently but the object can also occur at the beginning of the sentence, especially in the case of those which have no subject nominal,

e.g.   *Khasu limeneli ndinaligula kumsika* 'This (very) hoe I bought it at the market'

Note that the object *Khasu* is repeated by its concord *li* and then infixed in the verbal predicate as well, i.e. *ndina-li-gula*

This word order serves to put stress on the object.

Circumstantial Complements

Time, place and manner as syntactic markers, categorised here as circumstantial complements, are usually found at the beginning and at the end of a sentence.

Complements of time are mainly nouns of class 5 and class 6,

e.g. *Lelo lino tikayamba* 'this very day we start'

Analikudwala dzulo lija 'He was sick on that day'

Tsiku lina anawo anakomana mmawa 'That day those children met in the morning'

Complements of place belong as a rule to noun classes 16, 17 and 18 (see page 19),

e.g. *Ana anga abwela kwathu* 'My children went home'

Khalani pansi 'Sit on the floor'

Kodi ndani ali munyumba? 'Who is in the house?'

Complements of manner are often nominals of class 7,

e.g. *Aiphika nsima chikilukutu* 'She cooks the porridge hard and dry'

Anamusekela chipongwe 'They laughed at him derisively'

MULTIPLE SENTENCES

Multiple sentences are of two types: they are either a complex of verbal sentences, or of non-verbal plus verbal sentences.

Complex Verbal Sentences

These occur as strings usually joined by the conjunctive *na-* 'and' or the disjunctive *koma* 'but',

e.g. *Anafika kumudzi nadzola mafuta, nadulira mduliro, natha* 'They came

43

to the village and anointed themselves with oil, (and) shaved and finished.'

Anayesesa **koma** *sanachira.* 'He-tried-and-tried- but did not get better.'

A string without conjunctives can also occur, for example, as a sequence of imperatives:

e.g.   *Musamalimbana,* **lekani, paitani, kafuneni** *chimanga.* 'Don't quarrel, stop, go, go and look for maize.'

Verbs of Motion

Verbs like **-dza** come'; **-pita** go; **-bwema** 'remain' and **-tenga** take, often introduce a sequence of verbals. The tense/aspect markers **-dza-** and **-ka-** (see page 37) may be regarded as a subdivision of this verb class,

e.g.   *Nthondo* **anapita kukapanga** *minoma* 'Nthondo went to make beehives'

Anacoka kukakhala *ku dziko la mapili* **kutsata** *chimanga.* 'He went away to live in the hill country and look for maize.'

Speech and cognition verbs

Examples of these are **-ti** say; **-iza** 'tell'; **-ankha** 'answer'; **-funsa** 'ask'; **-mva** hear; **-ona** 'see'.

These may occur with an objectival clause, often introduced by the conjunction **kuti** 'that',

e.g.   *Anandiuza* **kuti nkhuku zonse zinafa.** 'He told me that all the chickens died'

Onani **kuti ukamadya nsima ndiwo ndi dzombe.** 'Look, you have eaten porridge with grasshopper relish.'

Verbs such as *-yamba* 'begin', *-leka* 'stop' and *-funa* 'want' occur with objectival clauses in which the second verb occurs in the infinitive form,

e.g.   *Ndifuna **kumathandiza** amai anga.* 'I (always) want to help my mother.'

       *Sanafunadi **kukwatiwa**.* 'She did not at all want to be married'

       *Analikuleka **kulila** namamvera nyimbo.* 'She stopped crying and listened to (those) songs.'

       *Anayamba **kukulapo**.* 'She started to grow up.'

A Non-Verbal and a Verbal Clause

These usually follow each other in the following order without a connector:

e.g.   **Cabwino, ndamva**. 'It is all right, I understand'

       Si lelo, adzapita *loweluka.* 'Not to-day, they will go on Saturday.'

Initial Invariable Words

Sections of a complex sentence may be marked by initial invariable words like *ngakhale* 'even if, although'; *kapena* 'if'; *chifukwa cha-* 'because of'; *kaamba akuti* 'on account of'; *mpaka* 'after'; *tsono* 'perhaps';

e.g.   **Ngakhale** *Nchowa analikuyenda mumtima mwache munali nkhondo.* 'Even though Nchowa used to go (there), there was war (evil) in her (his) heart'.

       *Amai anali ndi cisoni **chifukwa chakusowa** malo.* 'The mother is sad because there was no place to sleep.'

       *Maloto amenewa ndi abwino **akuti** musaone m'mene tasaukira leromu.* 'These dreams are good because you do not see in them how miserable we are at present.'

       Mpaka *atayenda masiku ena anai munyamata wina anayamba kumva* *litsipa.* 'After he had walked these four days the young man began to feel his head swell.'

Sequence of Tense Markers

The sequence of tense markers *-ta-* and *-na-* (see page 36) occurs in complex verbal sentences and indicates that the first action was completed when the others happened,

e.g.   *Atatsitiza anawalipira* 'After they had finished, he paid them.'

   Atayenda nthawi anafika kumtsinje wamadzi. 'When he had walked for some time he came to a stream of water.'

The Aspect Marker *-ka-*

This only occurs in a multiverbal sentence introducing a condition (see pages 36-37),

e.g.   *Tikafuna kuphunzila Cinyanja mudzatiphunzitsa?* 'If we want to learn Cinyanja, will you help us?'

   Mukacoka pano mupita kwamfumu. 'When you leave here go to the chief.'

CAVEAT

Sentences which are considerably longer than those quoted above have been found in tape recorded speech as well as in written literature. However not enough research has been done to make it possible to describe these.

A detailed study of Nyanja syntax as well as that of the phonology and the dialects of Cinyanja is yet to be undertaken and it is hoped that this modest outline is a prelude to such studies.

BIBLIOGRAPHY

Atkins, G. (1950) 'The Parts of Speech in Nyanja'. *The Nyasaland Journal,* Vol. III, No. 1 (January) pp 7-58.

Atkins, G. (1950) 'Suggestions for an Amended Spelling and Word Division of Nyanja'. *Africa* Vol. XX No.3 (July) pp 200-218.

Burke, S. J. (1969) 'A Spectrographic study of some tonal minimal pairs in ChiChewa'. In manuscript, Blantyre, Malawi.

Givon, Talmy (1970) 'An outline of the Grammatical Structure of Central Bantu Languages: A Field Manual'. In manuscript.

Ntara, S. J. (1964) *Ncowa.* Longman East Africa.

Ntara, S. J. (1966) *Nthondo.* Nkoma

Ohannessian, Sirarpi & Mubanga E. Kashoki (Eds.) (1978) *language in Zambia.* International African Institute, London.

Price, T. (1953) *The Elements of Nyanja for English-speaking Students.* Church of Scotland Mission, Blantyre, Nyasaland.

Scott & Hetherwick (1957) *Dictionary of the Nyanja language.* USCL. London.

Stevick, E. W. (1965) *CiNyanja Basic Course.* Washington D.C., Foreign Services Institute.

Thompson, T. D. (1955) *A practical approach to ChiNyanja.* Government Printer, Zomba.

Watkins, M. H. (1933) *Grammar of ChiCewa.* Philadelphia Linguistic Society of America.

Whitely, W. H. (1966) *A Study of Yao Sentences.* Oxford University Press, Oxford.

Whitely, W. H. (1969) *ChiCewa Intensive Course.* Likuni Press, Lilongwe, Malawi.